*Primarily Speaking:*

# LDS CLIP ART

BOOK TWO

*Primarily Speaking:*

# LDS CLIP ART

BOOK TWO

Joanna Lewis    Brenda Luther

Bookcraft
Salt Lake City, Utah

Copyright © 1990 by Bookcraft, Inc.

All rights reserved. Permission is hereby granted *with purchase* to reproduce any part of this book on a limited basis for personal use only. Reproduction of any part of this book for commercial use is expressly forbidden. Bookcraft is a registered trademark of Bookcraft, Inc., 1848 West 2300 South, Salt Lake City, Utah, 84119.

ISBN 0-88494-751-3

3rd Printing, 1993

Printed in the United States of America

*Everything we are or ever hope to become
we owe to four wonderful people:
John and Eleanor Norgail
and
Frank and Margaret Skidmore.
To these we dedicate this book with all
the love they've given us over the years.*

*Love ya, Mom and Dad.*

# INSTRUCTIONS

As with our first book, this book is full of fun and interesting pictures, words, and borders that can be used in a variety of different ways. Use them to make invitations for parties, meetings, or showers. Personalize your own thank-you notes, stationery or place cards. They are perfect for programs, favors, flyers, or certificates. Enlarge the pictures for use as visual aids for stories, songs, or lessons. They can also be enlarged for posters or bulletin boards. Use your imagination, and the possibilities are almost endless!

To use this book:

1. Decide on a project.
2. Make a clear copy of the page(s) you will be using.
3. Cut out the pictures and words to be used.
4. Lay out your project on graph paper.
5. Tape everything in place.
6. Have copies made of your completed project. (Colored paper is fun!)

We have added a few new ideas to this book that will require the following instructions:

### DOOR SIGNS:

There are door signs for each Primary class (including Nursery), each Young Women class, one for Relief Society, and one for Home Evening. These door signs will be fun and practical to use at church and at home. Just copy onto cardstock paper the door signs desired. Color and laminate, then cut them out around the dark lines. Cut along the dotted lines also. (This will enable you to hang your door signs on any door knob.)

### PENCIL-TOPPERS:

There are pencil-toppers for all Primary and Young Women classes. They can be given to the students or kept to be used in class. All you do is copy on cardstock paper, color and laminate, cut out, and hot-glue onto a pencil. These pencil-toppers would make cute badges too.

### NAME-TAGS, AWARDS AND BOOKMARKS:

There are some darling name-tags, awards, and bookmarks that will be very useful to you dedicated Primary workers. Copy them as needed for your personal use.

BLANK GAME BOARD:

This blank game board will enable you to make a game out of any subject you are trying to teach. All you do is make a copy of both pages and mount the two pages side by side in a file folder. In this form it may be labeled and filed easily. Use your imagination and fill it in as desired. Color and laminate if desired. Make your own game cards by using the blank card page provided. Make as many as needed, then laminate and cut out. Store them with your game folder. This game board can be used over and over again, and will provide lots of fun for all.

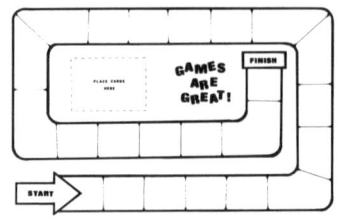

Important note:

Make copies of the pages you wish to use. Do not use the original! Then you will be able to use the book over and over again.

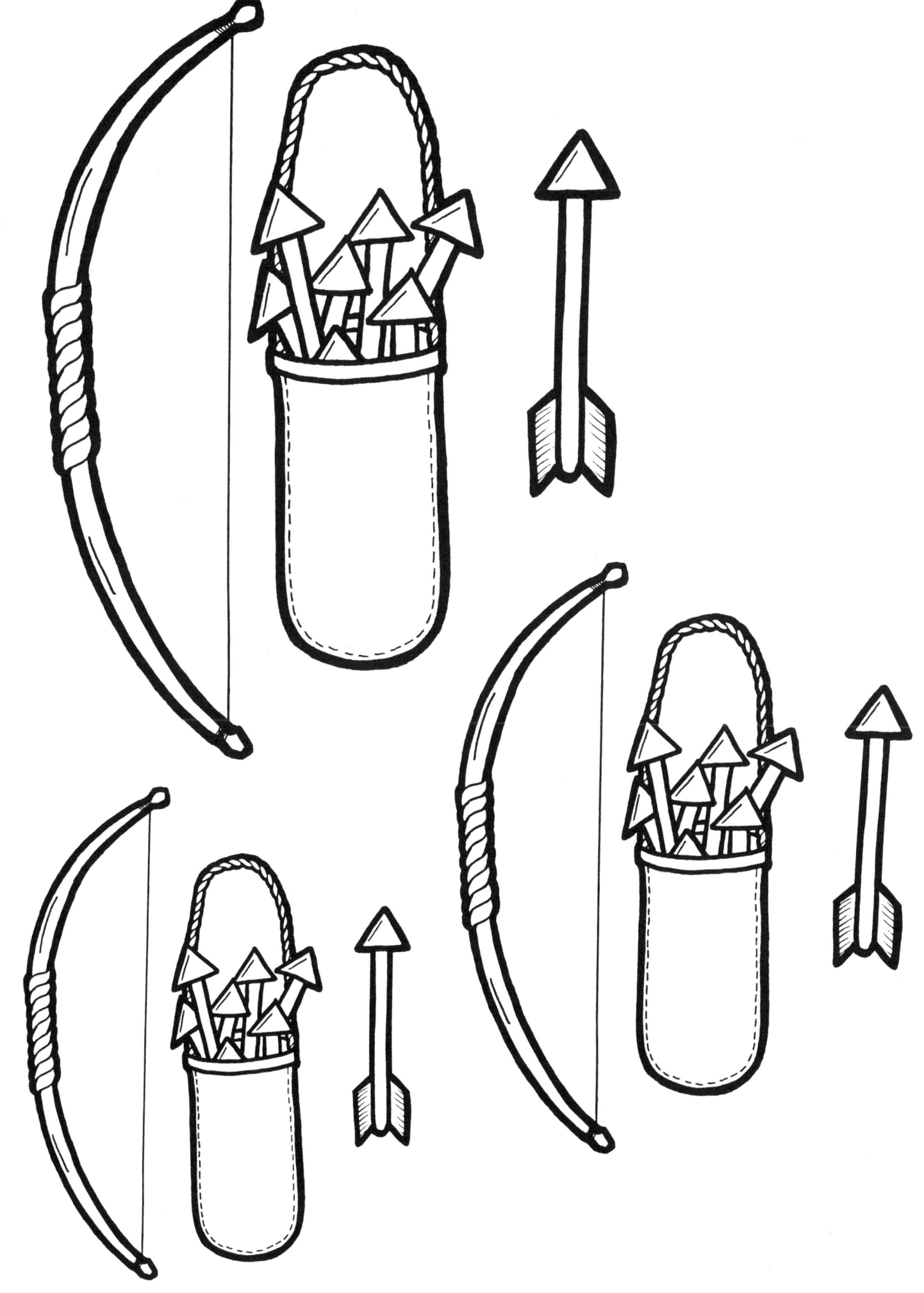

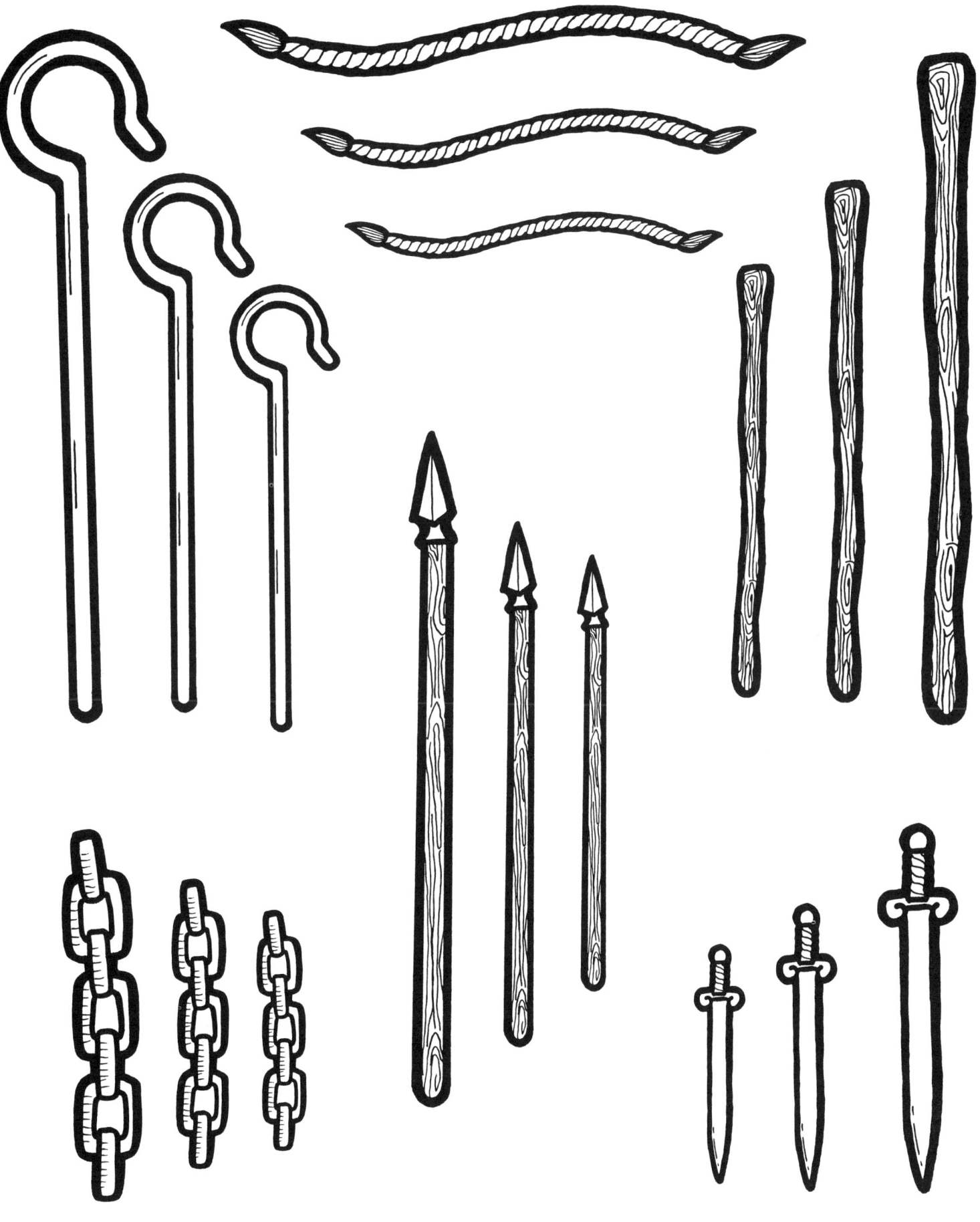

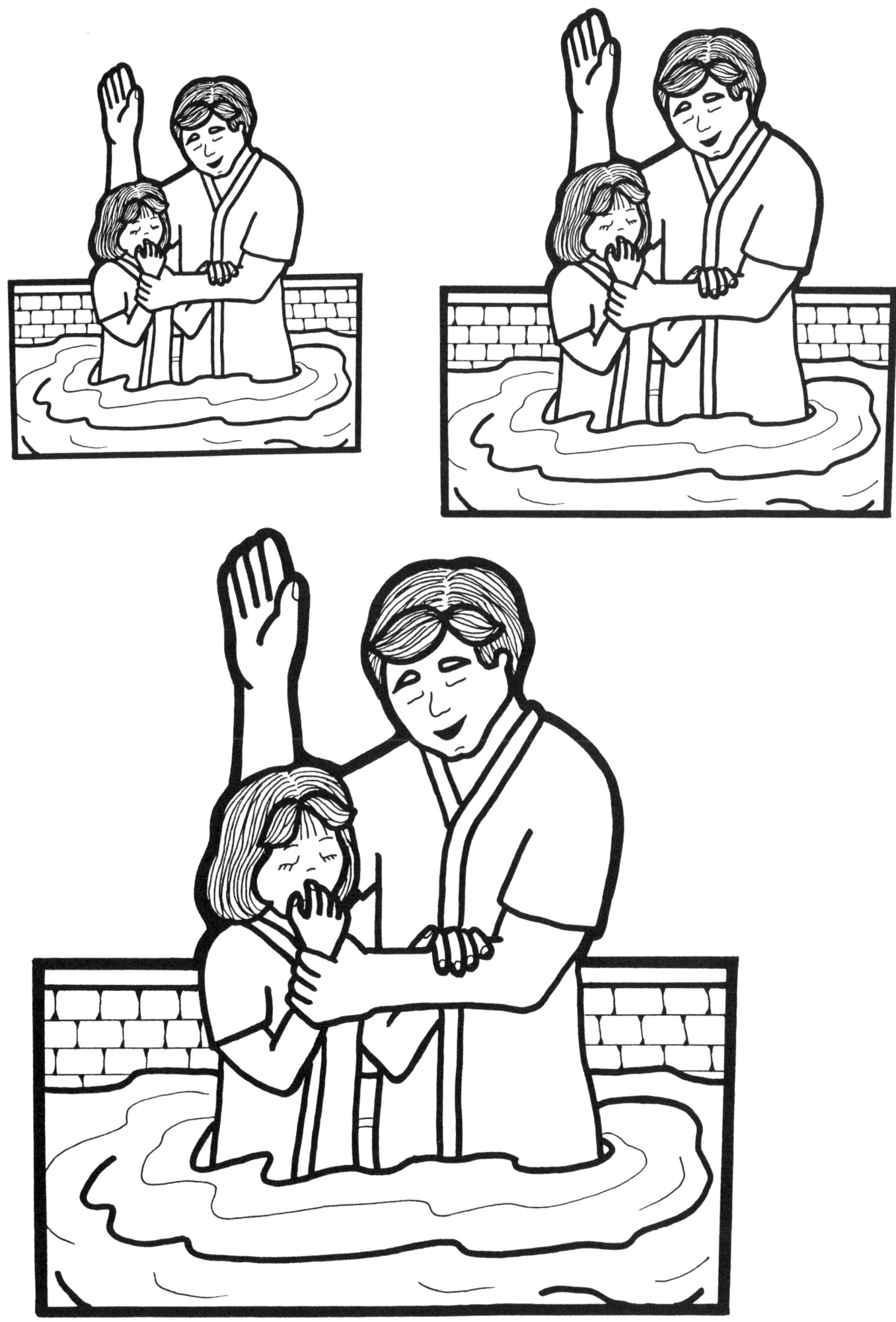

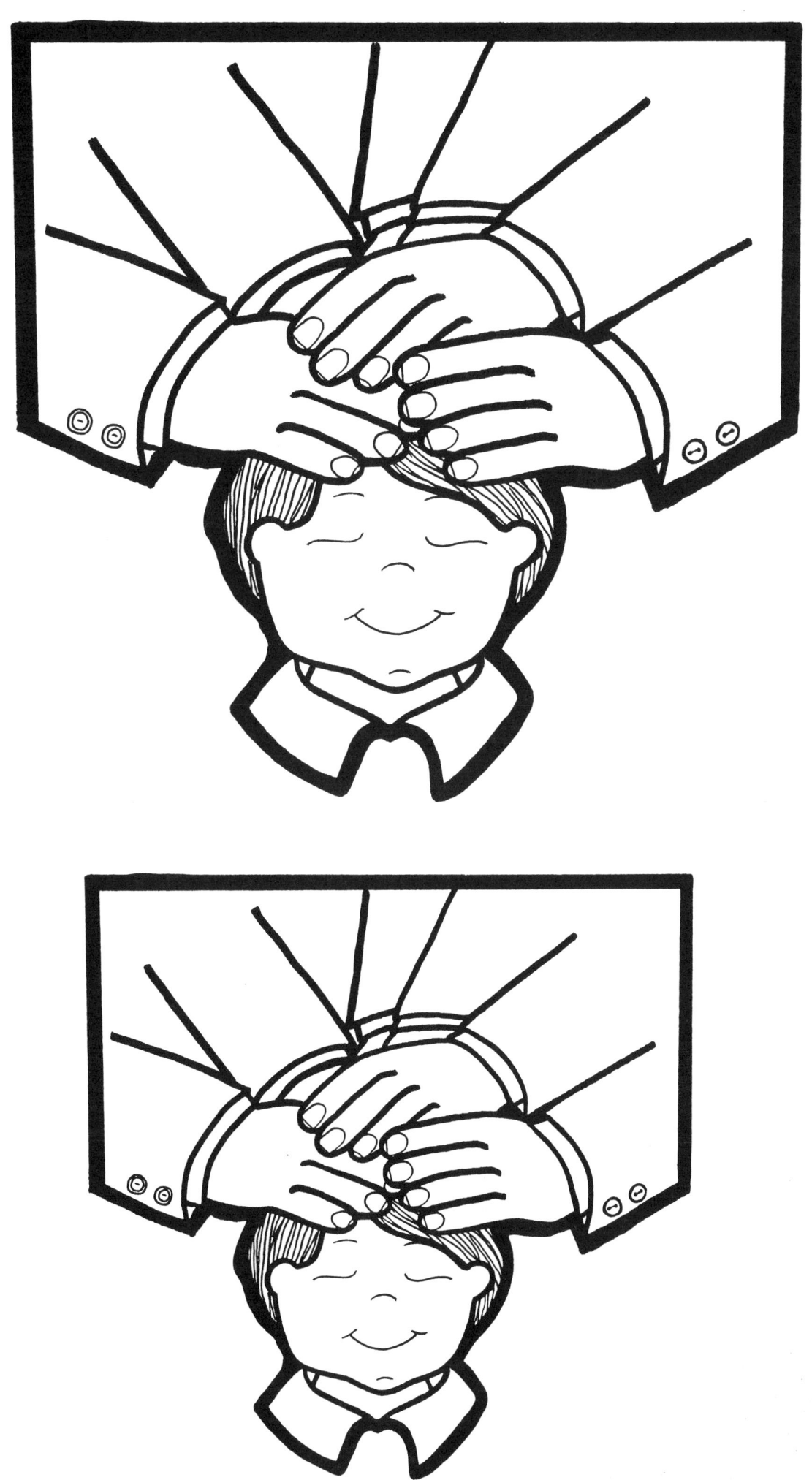

HURRAY FOR SCOUTS

PARTICIPATION AWARD TO

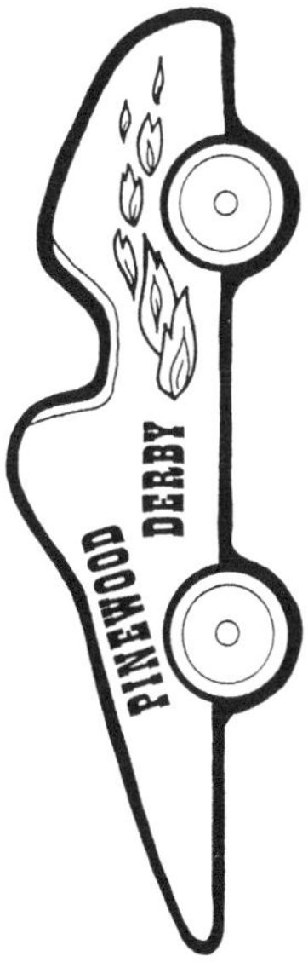

Your Car Was Most

# MILLION DOLLAR SCOUT

_____ has proven he's worth a million dollars to our pack.

For _____.

WAY TO GO!!

_____   _____
Date             Den Leader

I Was a
"Hoppy" Helper
In Primary Today

MY NAME IS:

NURSERY

**Sunbeam**

Jesus Wants Me For a Sunbeam

MY NAME IS:

I was a "SHINING" helper in Primary!!!!

Star B

*I can*

CHOOSE

THE

RIGHT

CTR A

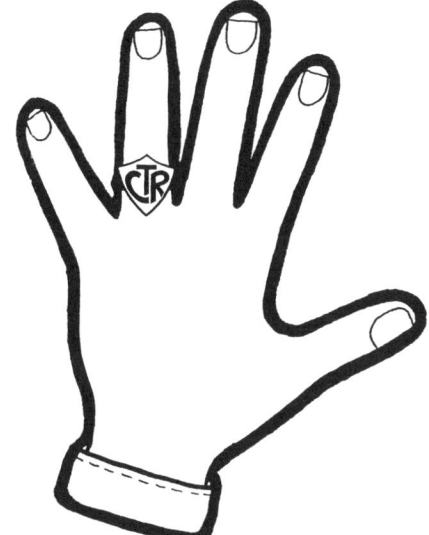

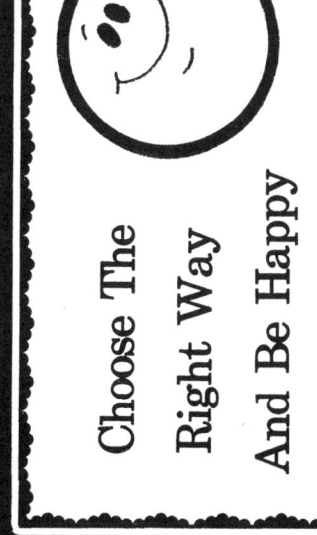

# Valiant A

I Can

Follow

God's

Plan

For Me

# Merrie Miss A

I Can Prepare To Receive The Priesthood

# Blazer A

# SPECIAL RECOGNITION

To _____

*who completed all the requirements
for the Gospel in Action Award.*

*You did a super job!!*

*Congratulations*

_____
*Teacher*

_____
*Date*

# CONGRATULATIONS TO

_____

For Special Achievement in the Young Women Organization.

_____

Signed _____    Date _____

---

Stand For Truth And Righteousness 🔥 Stand For Truth And Righteousness 🔥 Stand For Truth And Righteousness 🔥 Stand For Truth And Righteousness

**BEEHIVE**

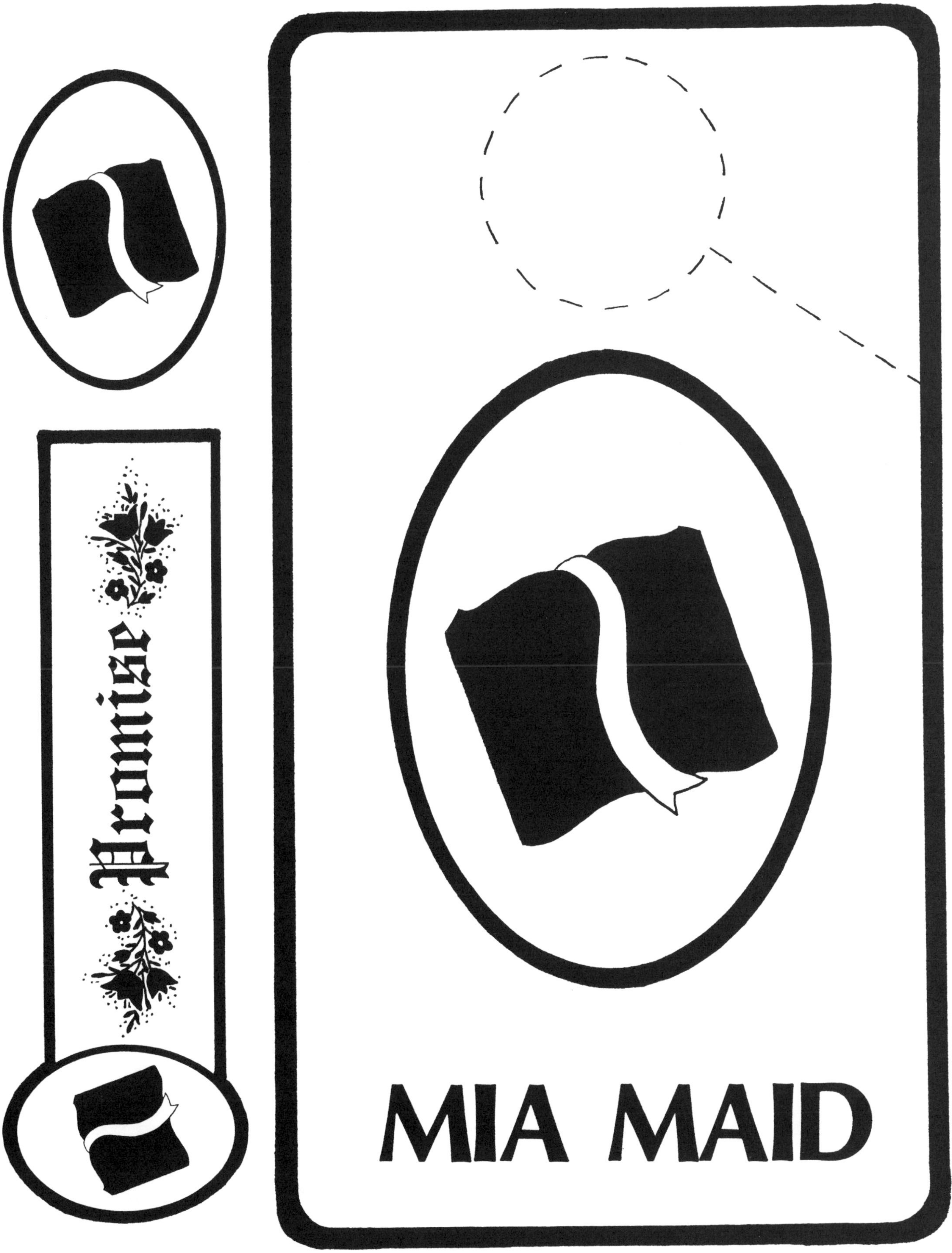

MIA MAID

LAUREL

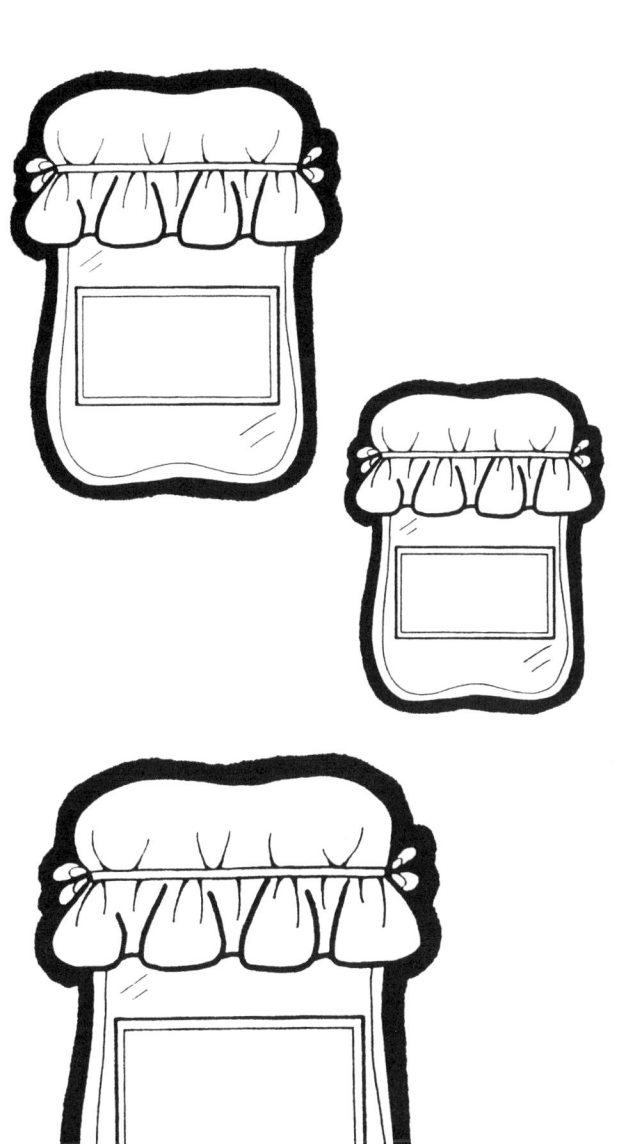

 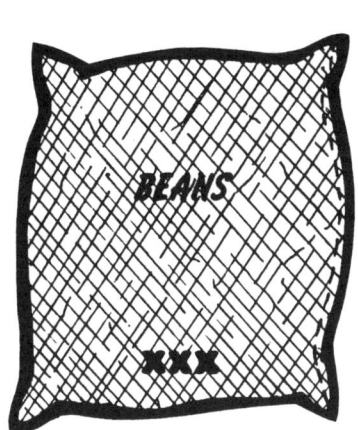 

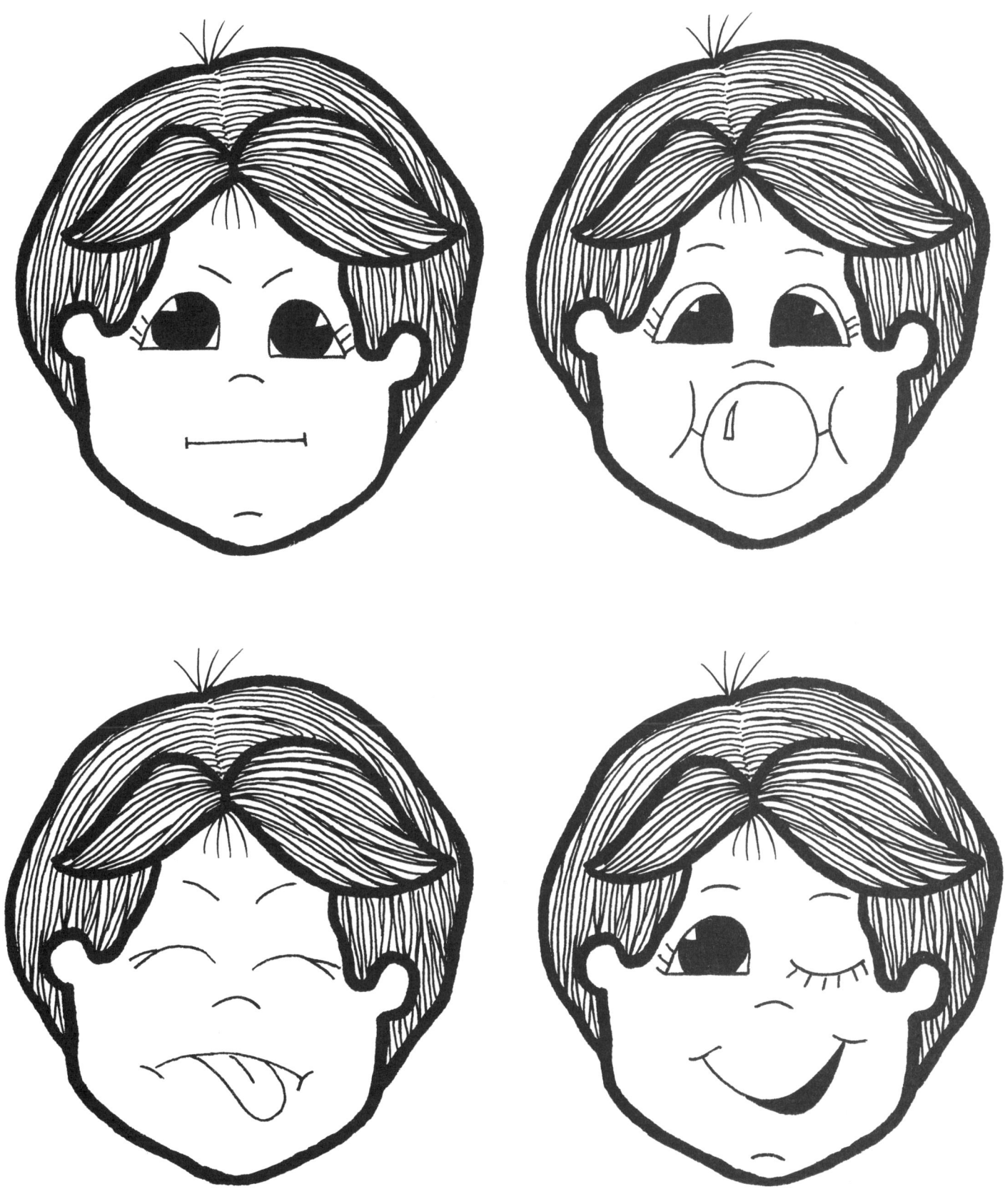

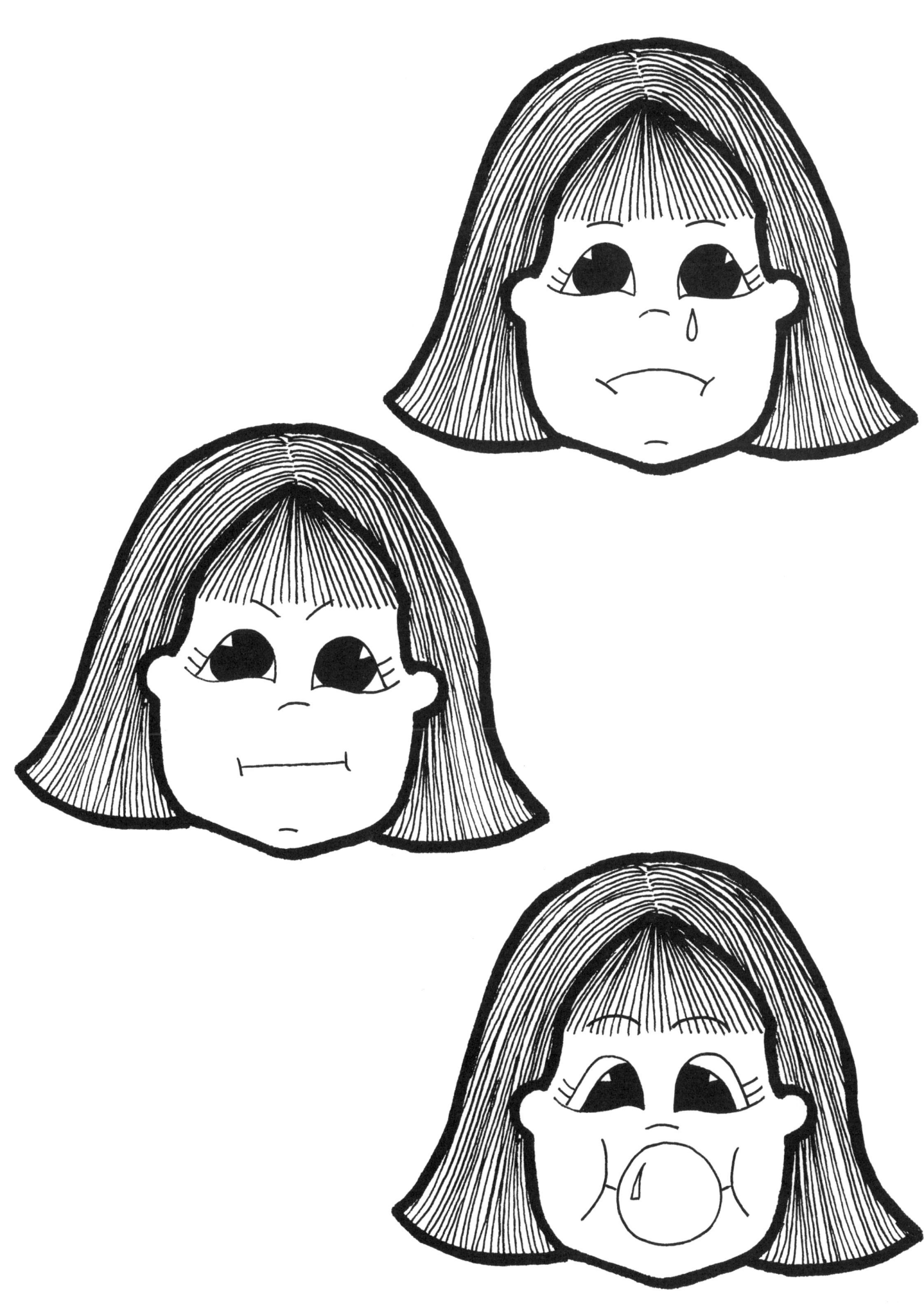

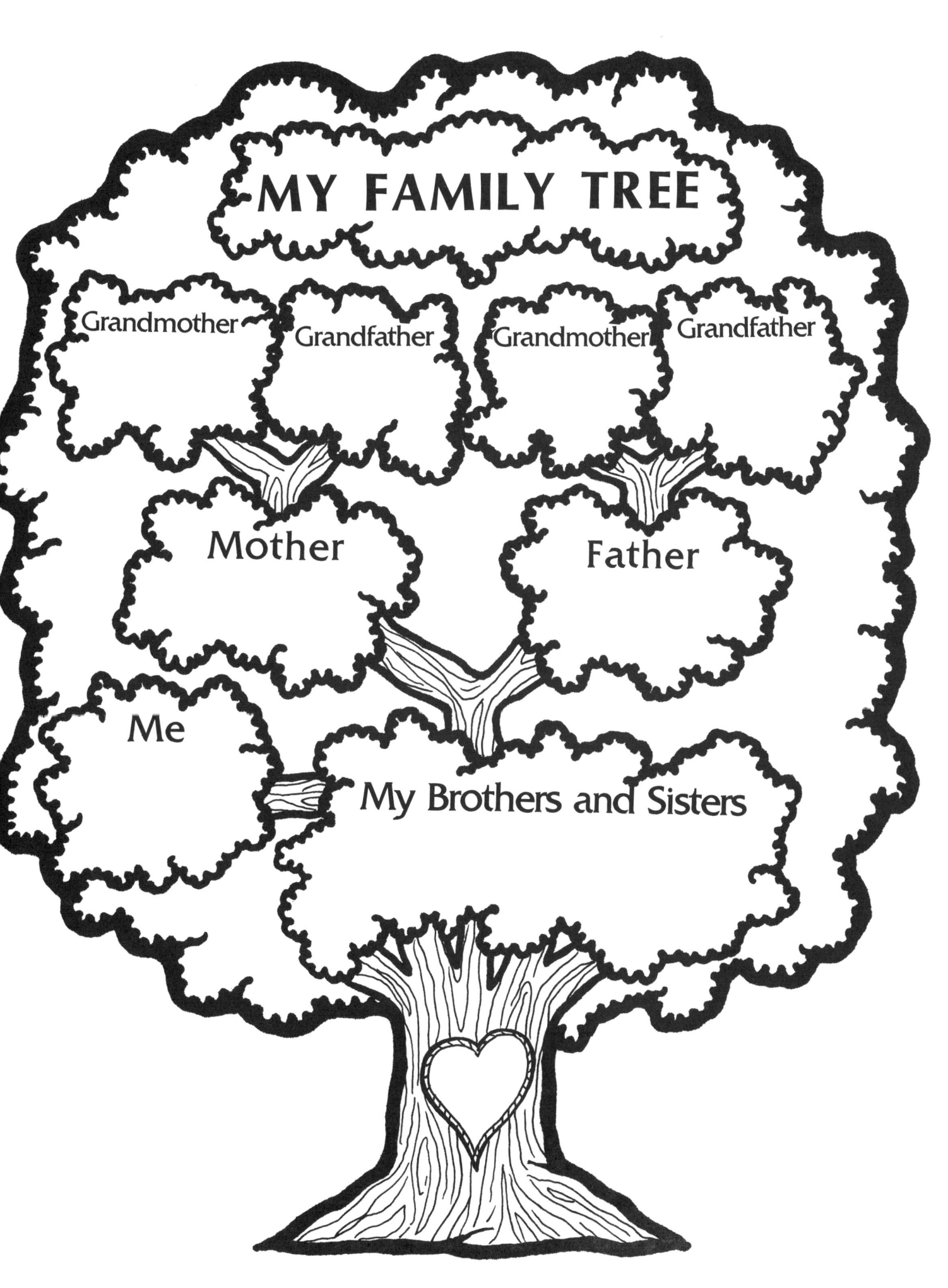

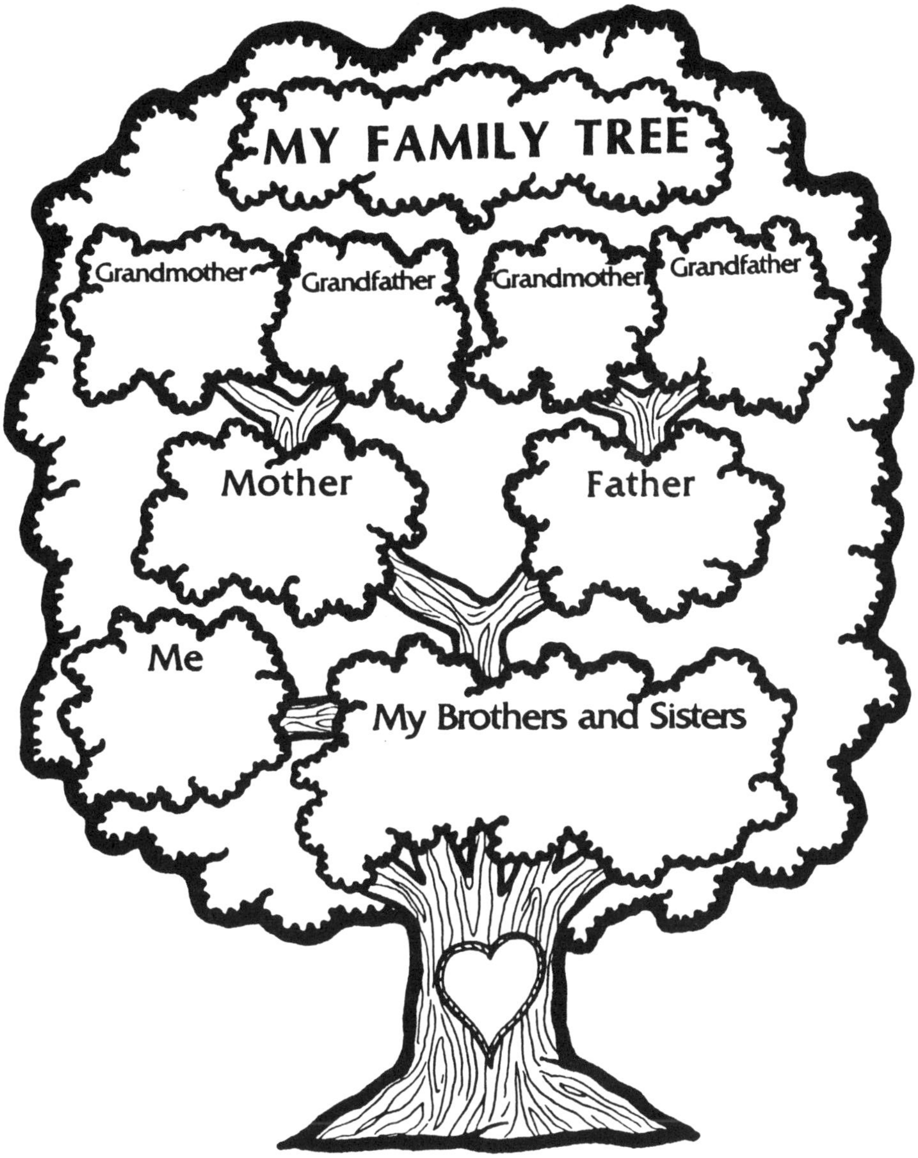

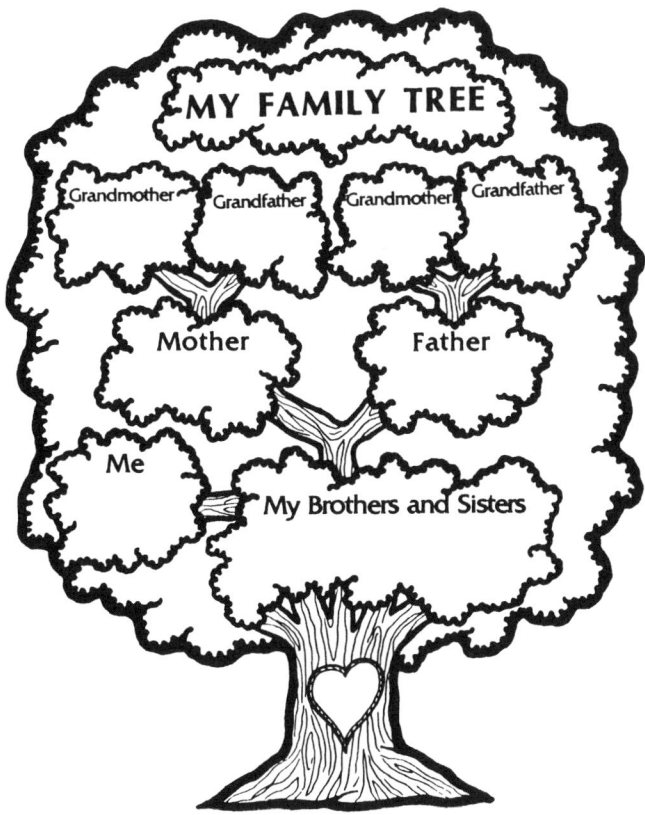
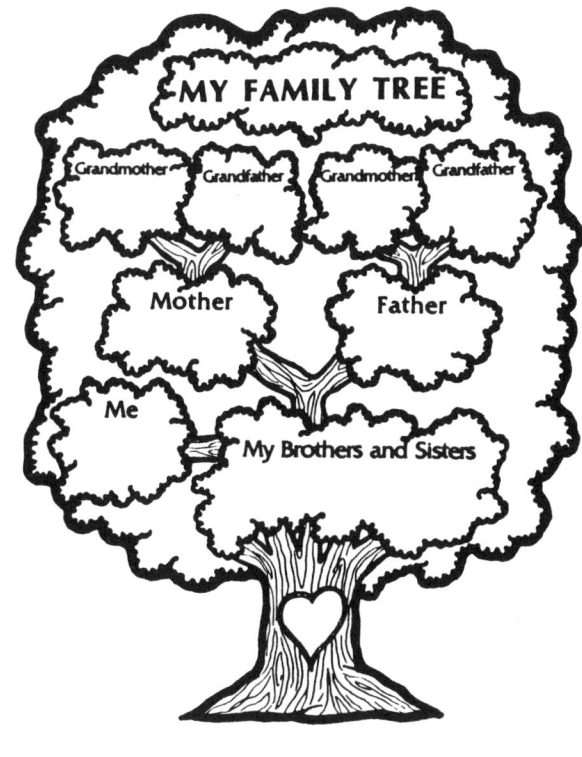

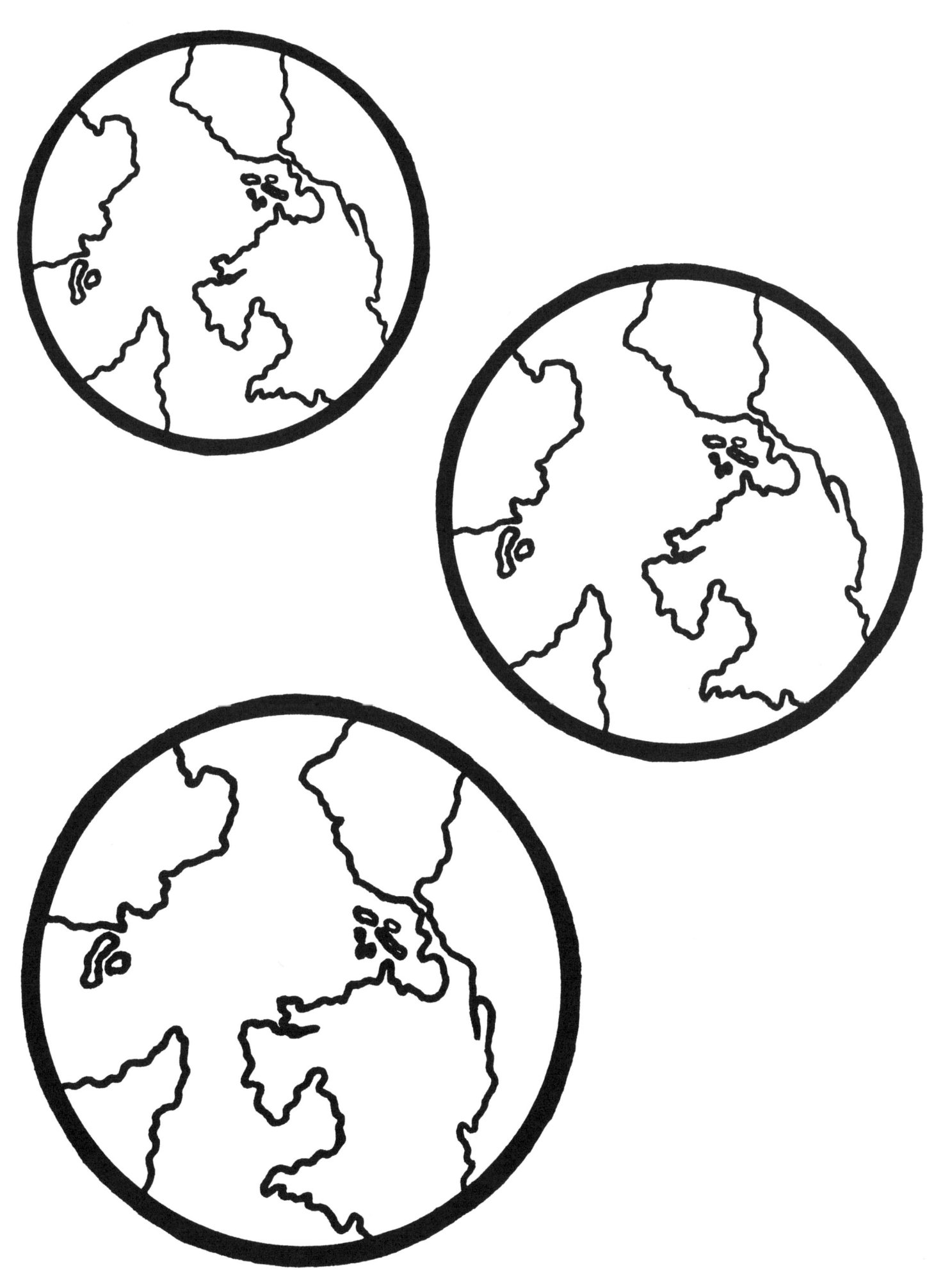

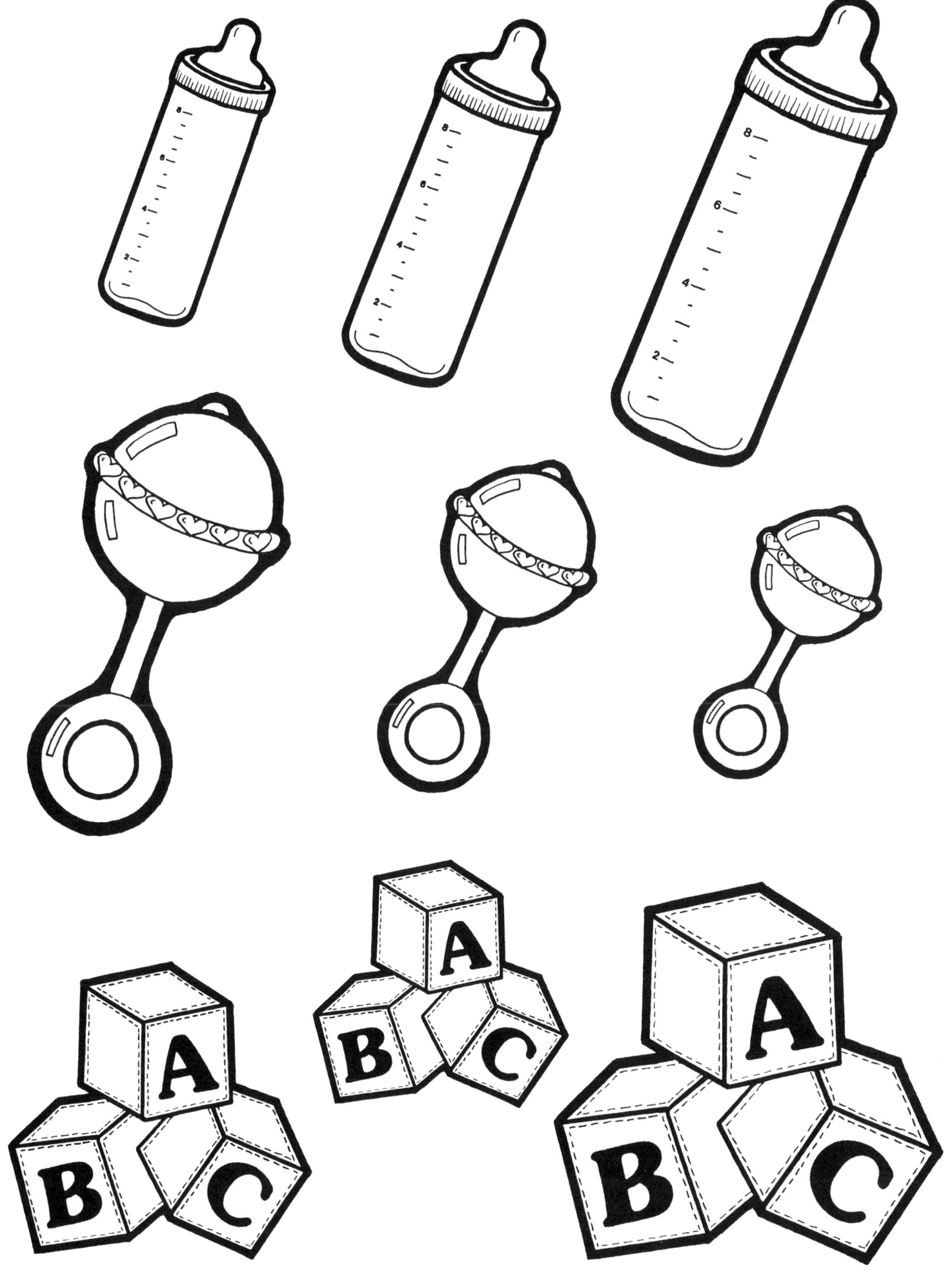

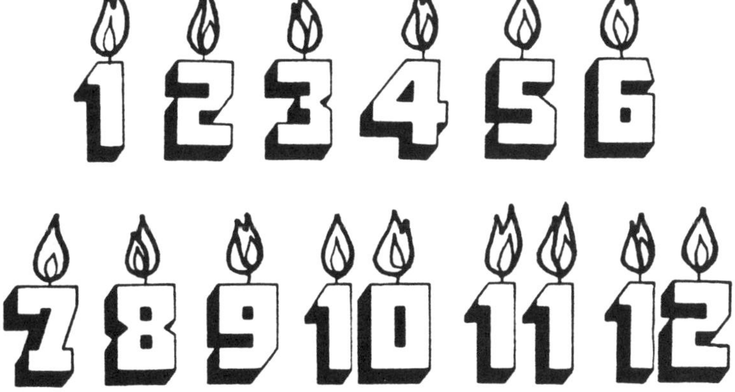

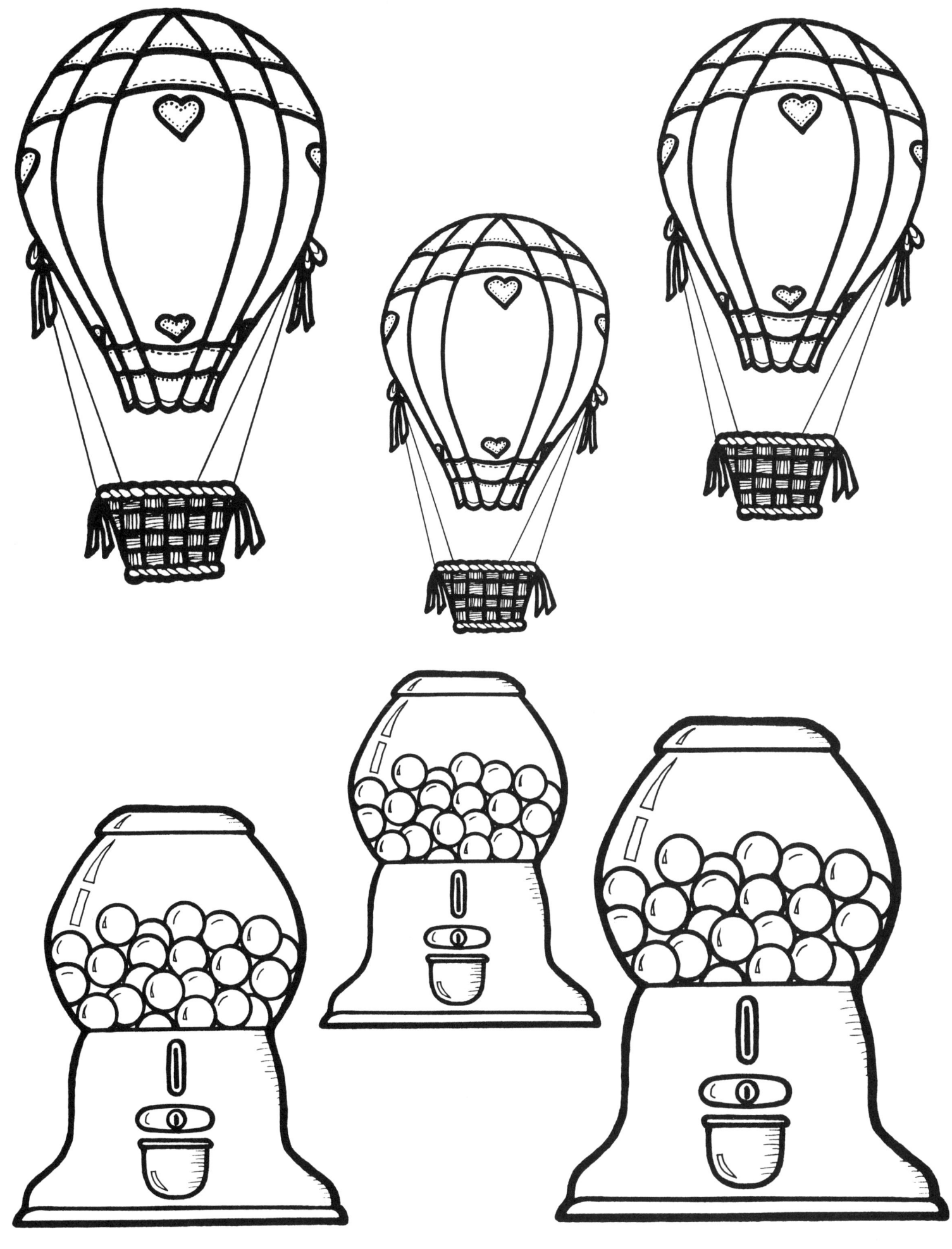

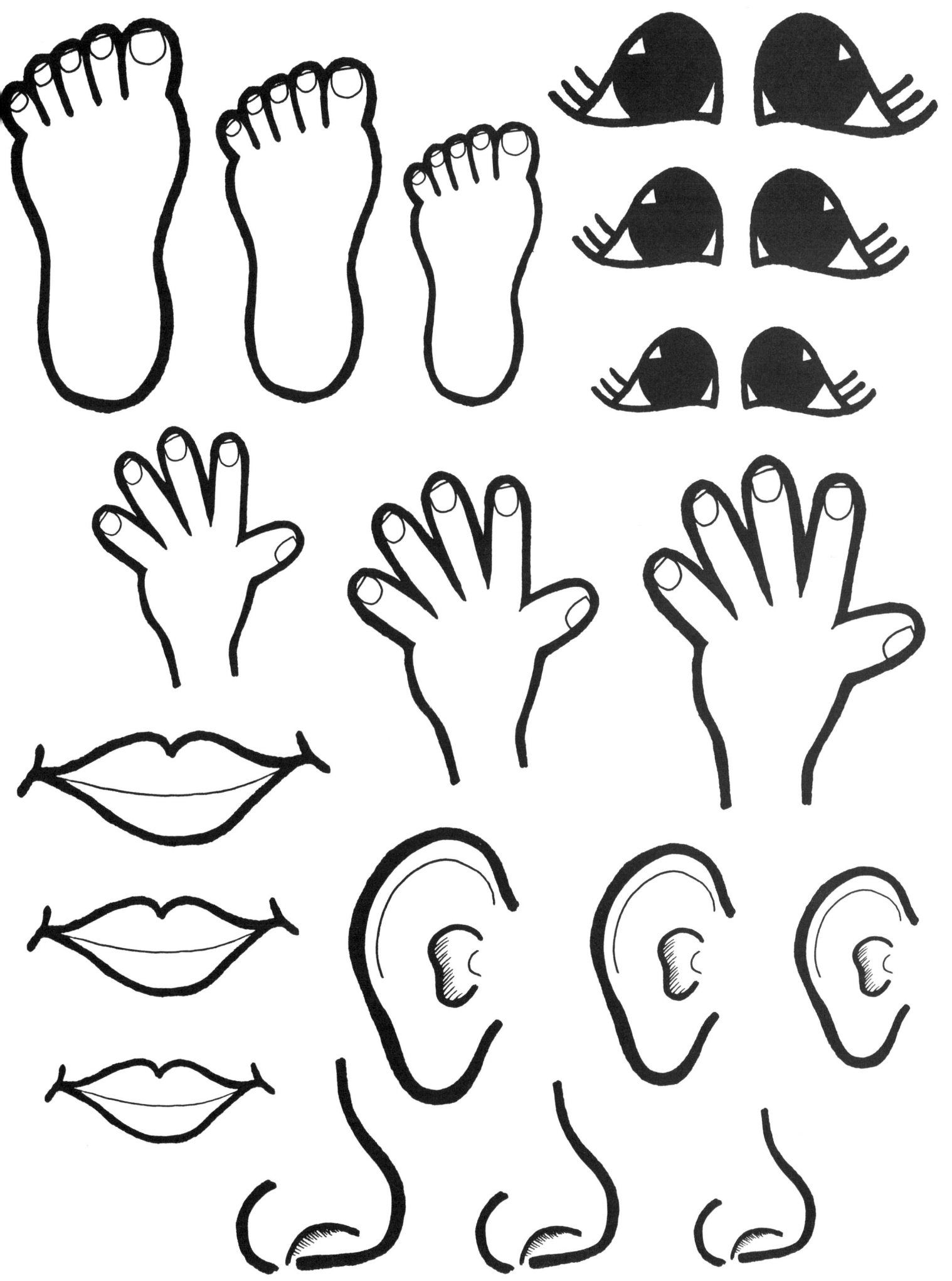

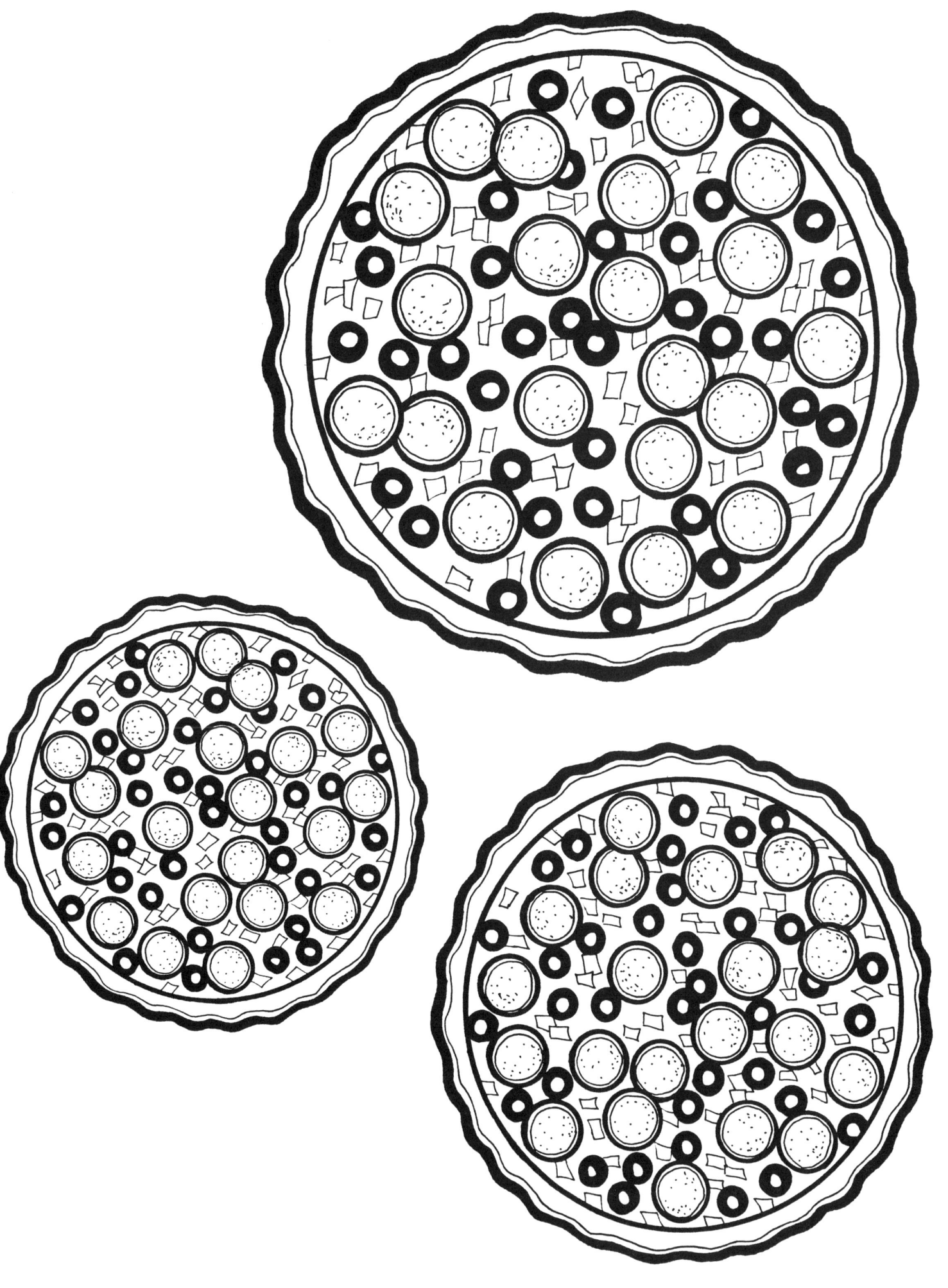

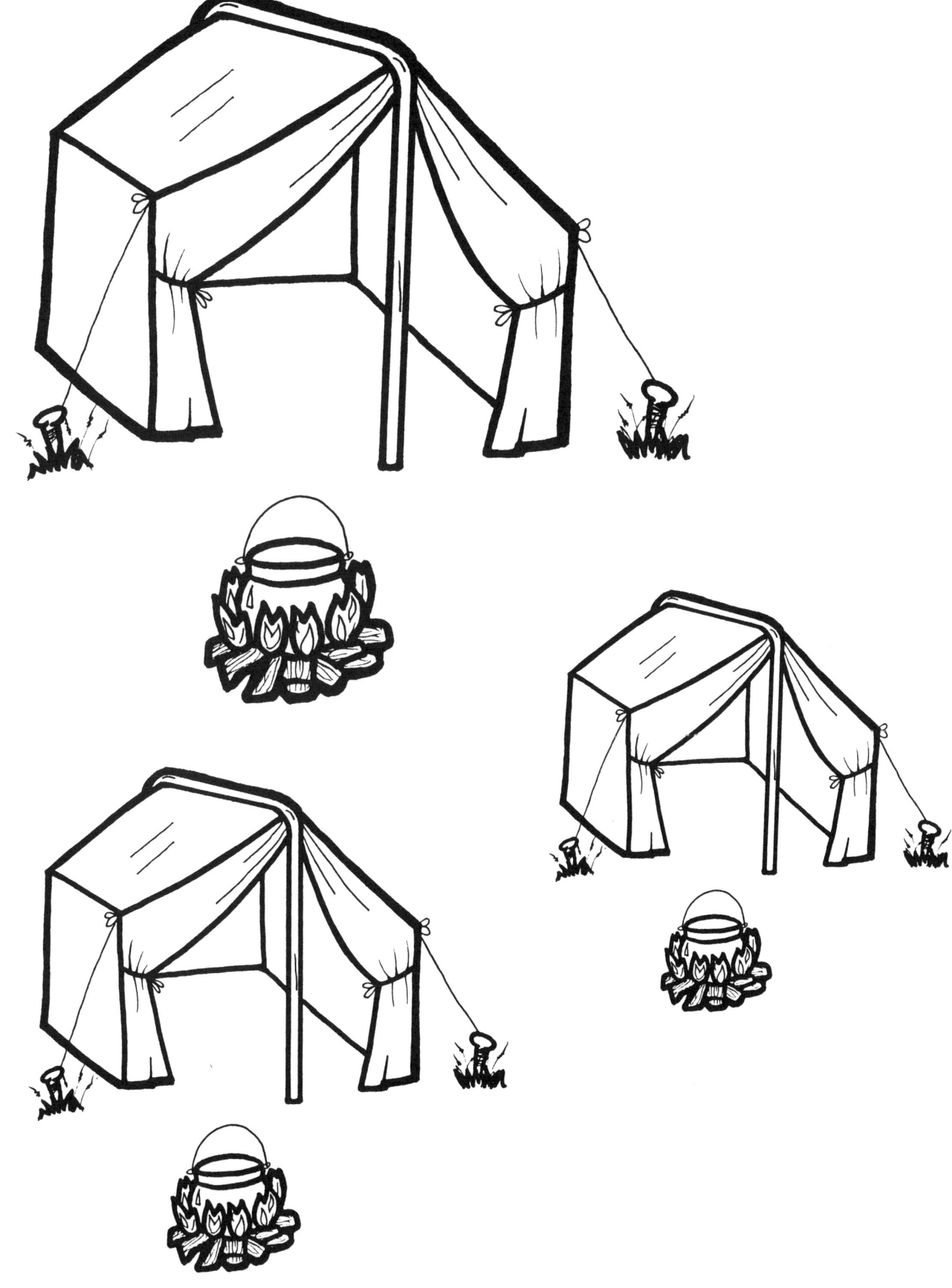

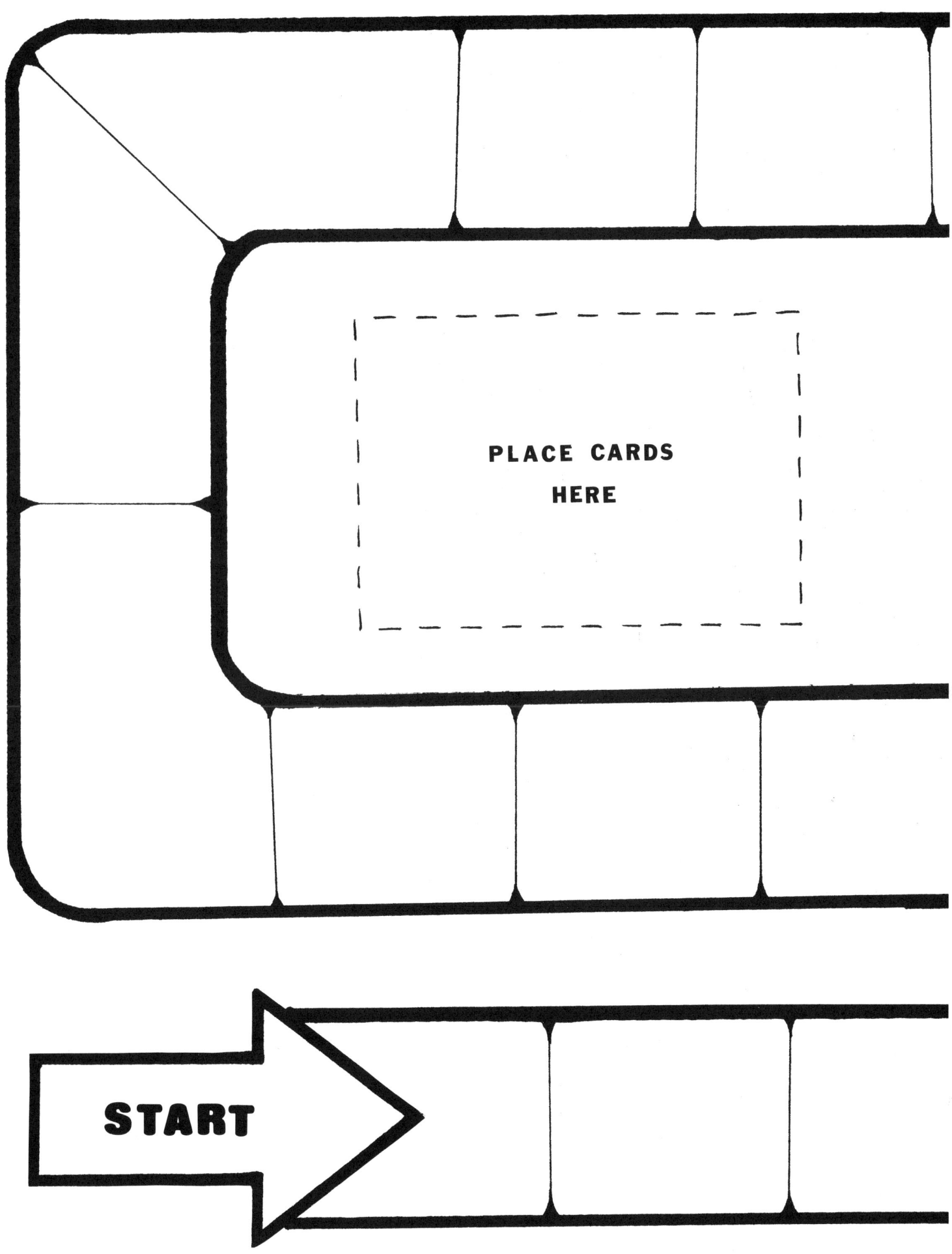

# BLANK GAME CARDS

# GIFT TAGS

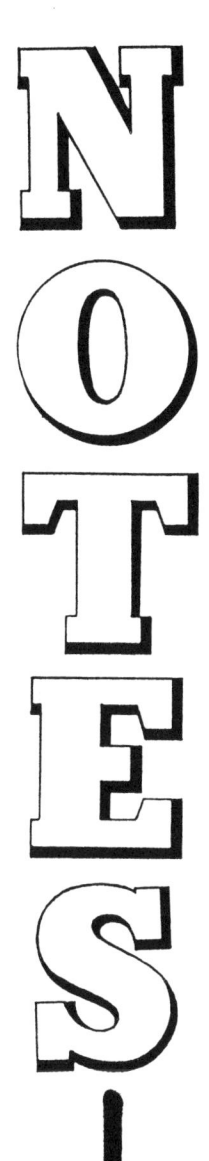

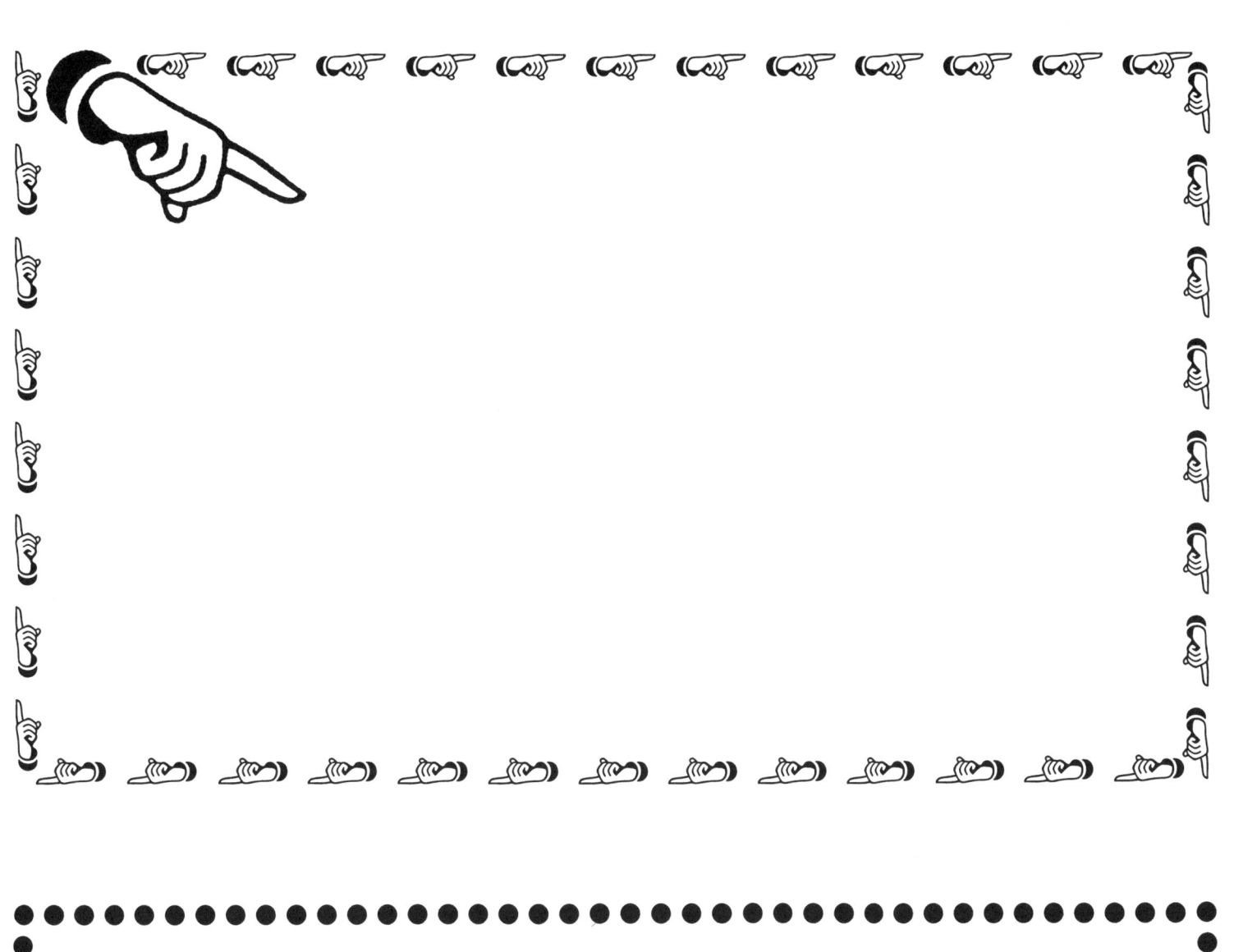

# INVITATION

## THANK YOU
### THANK YOU
### THANK YOU

# MERRIE MISS MEMORANDUM

# MERRIE MISS MEMORANDUM

# MERRIE MISS MEMORANDUM

# BLAZER BRIEFING

# BLAZER BRIEFING

# BLAZER BRIEFING

SUNBEAM
SUNBEAM
SUNBEAM

STAR A
STAR A
STAR A

STAR B
STAR B
STAR B

VALIANT A
VALIANT A
VALIANT A

CTR A
CTR A
CTR A

VALIANT B
VALIANT B
VALIANT B

COURSE 11
COURSE 11
COURSE 11

BLAZER A
BLAZER A
BLAZER A

CTR B
CTR B
CTR B

MERRIE MISS A
MERRIE MISS A
MERRIE MISS A

# I LOVE PRIMARY
## I LOVE PRIMARY
### I LOVE PRIMARY

**Cub Scouts**

**Cub Scouts**

**Cub Scouts**

***PINEWOOD DERBY***

***PINEWOOD DERBY***

***PINEWOOD DERBY***

NURSERY

**NURSERY**

**NURSERY**

Early Bird Breakfast

Early Bird Breakfast

Early Bird Breakfast

Blue & Gold Banquet

Blue & Gold Banquet

Blue & Gold Banquet

# ICE CREAM SOCIAL
## ICE CREAM SOCIAL
### ICE CREAM SOCIAL

JOURNALS

JOURNALS

JOURNALS

Teacher's Helper

Teacher's Helper

Teacher's Helper

**Primary Softball**

**Primary Softball**

**Primary Softball**

Primary News

Primary News

Primary News

**SHARING TIME**

**SHARING TIME**

**SHARING TIME**

*Miss And Her Mom Party*

*Miss And Her Mom Party*

*Miss And Her Mom Party*

Daddy Daughter Date

Daddy Daughter Date

Daddy Daughter Date

Primary Activity Day

Primary Activity Day

Primary Activity Day

*Sacrament Meeting Presentation*

*Sacrament Meeting Presentation*

*Sacrament Meeting Presentation*

I'm a member of the L.D.S. church!!

I'm a member of the L.D.S. church!!

I'm a member of the L.D.S. church!!

*I'm Getting Baptized*

*I'm Getting Baptized*

*I'm Getting Baptized*

# Relief Society News

**FOOD STORAGE**

**FOOD STORAGE**

**FOOD STORAGE**

Relief Society News

Relief Society News

𝕳ome 𝕴s 𝖂here 𝖂he 𝕳eart 𝕴s

𝕳ome 𝕴s 𝖂here 𝖂he 𝕳eart 𝕴s

**𝕳ome 𝕴s 𝖂here 𝖂he 𝕳eart 𝕴s**

Home And Family Education

Home And Family Education

## Home And Family Education

## Compassionate Service/Social Relations

Compassionate Service/Social Relations

Compassionate Service/Social Relations

Home Management

Home Management

## Home Management

## Spiritual Living

Spiritual Living

Spiritual Living

HOMEMAKING

HOMEMAKING

HOMEMAKING

# For Time and All Eternity
## For Time and All Eternity
### For Time and All Eternity

### Bishopric's Message
## Bishopric's Message
# Bishopric's Message

# EVERY MEMBER A MISSIONARY
## EVERY MEMBER A MISSIONARY
### EVERY MEMBER A MISSIONARY

Set Your Goals High and Rise To Them
## Set Your Goals High and Rise To Them
## Set Your Goals High and Rise To Them

### *BEEHIVE*
## *BEEHIVE*
# *BEEHIVE*

# *MIA MAID*
## *MIA MAID*
### *MIA MAID*

*Stand For Truth and Righteousness*
## *Stand For Truth and Righteousness*
### *Stand For Truth and Righteousness*

### *LAUREL*
## *LAUREL*
# *LAUREL*

The Laying on of Hands
## The Laying on of Hands
# The Laying on of Hands

# Sunday School News

## Sunday School News

### Sunday School News

*Come Unto Christ*

*Come Unto Christ*

***Come Unto Christ***

# Proclaim The Gospel

## Proclaim The Gospel

Proclaim The Gospel

### Perfect The Saints

## Perfect The Saints

# Perfect The Saints

# Redeem The Dead

## Redeem The Dead

Redeem The Dead

*Happy Mother's Day*

*Happy Mother's Day*

***Happy Mother's Day***

## Happy Father's Day

Happy Father's Day

### Happy Father's Day

*ROSTER*

**ROSTER**

# ROSTER

CLASS RULES

## CLASS RULES

# CLASS RULES

# Priesthood News
## Priesthood News
### Priesthood News

Elder
Elder
Elder

High Priest
High Priest
High Priest

Deacon
Deacon
Deacon

Priest
Priest
Priest

Teacher
Teacher
Teacher

Priesthood Preview
Priesthood Preview
Priesthood Preview

☆ COURT OF HONOR ☆
☆ COURT OF HONOR ☆
☆ COURT OF HONOR ☆

WE MISSED YOU
WE MISSED YOU
WE MISSED YOU

SPORTS
SPORTS
SPORTS

WARD CAMPOUT
WARD CAMPOUT
WARD CAMPOUT

Birthdays
Birthdays
Birthdays

Time:
Date:
Place:

Time:
Date:
Place:

Time:
Date:
Place:

Young Men News

Young Men News

Young Men News

Super Job

Super Job

Super Job

Young Women News

Young Women News

Young Women News

Sugar & Spice

Sugar & Spice

Sugar & Spice

You're a Winner!

You're a Winner!

You're a Winner!

—NEWS FLASH—

—NEWS FLASH—

—NEWS FLASH—

It's TIME for a PARTY!!!

It's TIME for a PARTY!!!

It's TIME for a PARTY!!!

Something Special Is Happening

Something Special Is Happening

Something Special Is Happening

# IT'S SHOWTIME
## IT'S SHOWTIME
### IT'S SHOWTIME

**FIRESIDE**

**FIRESIDE**

**FIRESIDE**

# FAMILY HISTORY
## FAMILY HISTORY
### FAMILY HISTORY

ROADSHOW

ROADSHOW

ROADSHOW

Get Well Soon!

**Get Well Soon!**

## Get Well Soon!

We Have a Baby Girl

We Have a Baby Boy

We Have a Baby Girl

## We Have a Baby Boy

We Have a Baby Girl

## We Have a Baby Boy

# GREAT NEWS
## GREAT NEWS
### GREAT NEWS

*SURPRISE*

*SURPRISE*

*SURPRISE*

With Love

## With Love

## With Love

FOR BABY

FOR BABY

FOR BABY

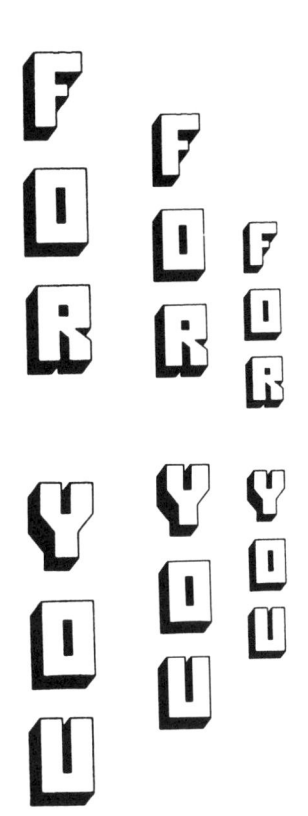

From All Of Us

From All Of Us

From All Of Us

*Love* *Love* *Love*

Especially For You

**Especially For You**

**Especially For You**

PARTY PARTY PARTY

HAPPY BIRTHDAY  HAPPY BIRTHDAY  HAPPY BIRTHDAY

BIRTHDAY PARTY!!

BIRTHDAY PARTY!!

BIRTHDAY PARTY!!

**EXCITING!**

**EXCITING!**

**EXCITING!**

There's No Place Like Home

There's No Place Like Home

There's No Place Like Home

# Upcoming Events

## Upcoming Events

### Upcoming Events

Best Wishes

Best Wishes

Best Wishes

The Time Has Come

**The Time Has Come**

**The Time Has Come**

Baptisms

Baptisms

Baptisms

A BIG THANKS!!

**A BIG THANKS!!**

**A BIG THANKS!!**

**PACK MEETING**

**PACK MEETING**

**PACK MEETING**

# Ward News

## Ward News

Ward News

New Ward Members

New Ward Members